AF439500

THE KAOMA THEOREM

JORDAN KIRK

THE KAOMA THEOREM

TEOREMA

THE KAOMA THEOREM
Jordan Kirk

© 2022 Jordan Kirk

All Rights Reserved.
Published by Teorema Press
Los Angeles, California
Printed in the United States of America

First Printing May 2022
ISBN 9-7988021049-1-0

Cover image: Albrecht Dürer, *The Men's Bath* (detail).

for C.

Les nombreuses parcelles de vérité qui sont répandues dans les œuvres des poètes ou des héros de l'Occident sont les restes d'initiations mariennes plus ou moins inachevées.

—Abdul-Hâdi

CONTENTS

THE LAUREATION OF THE
MOTHER TONGUE

One afternoon in California I fell asleep on my bed reading the first pages of the *Marriage of Philology and Mercury*. The back door of the house was open for the breeze. I don't know how long I'd been dozing when a noise startled me awake. It was coming from inside the room. It was October 22, 2018, and a pigeon was hopping around at the foot of the bed, churning the air with its wings and remonstrating with me.

Running my eye over the bookshelf one night in search of something to read, I realized that what I was looking for wouldn't be on the shelf. It wasn't anything I'd ever read; to my knowledge it did not yet exist. But everything about it was distinct in my memory. All that week a song had been stuck in my head, and I must have been murmuring along to it (the words are in a language I don't speak) as I stood there before the bookshelf. What I was looking for was a book about the discovery of a book. Such a book as could only be written by someone who had retrieved it from the site of its concealment.

Intellectual fascination with the metaphysics of youth.

Entanglement of mind across the disaster. Awareness recognizes and resumes awareness. The 'eminently telepathic phenomenon'. Spooky contemplation at a distance.

Do we want the whole neighborhood to know we are babysitters of the pure flame?

'If they haven't seen it before, they won't know what it is; if they have seen it, they won't care.' That's what my grandmother would say when I had to change my clothes in public.

The craftsmen of the vernacular have a custom. Rather than tell secrets they tell the properties of the languages in which they're told. They say there is a language made up not of names, like ours, but of passwords. It can pass as our language. Indeed, that is among its high honors. It can only be learned at the breast.

Fern is an emblem of finders. A tongue is a device for hearing mantra, a listening device. The book is a castle for its deity, a movable cathedral, an *itinerarium*.

The only idea is that you don't have to be fascinated by your thoughts.

'Athenya endaya.' —What is that, a name? —It's an iamb and an amphibrach. The *h* is silent.

Nothing is concealed. Everything is said outright, as plainly as possible. But what is being spoken about cannot be cognized, only recognized. And so the purport of the book remains elusive to all but those already experienced in the matter of the book.

To participate in a circuit of ferns dilates the certainty of being. Barren wind carving a wormhole in the tissue. A gossamer gland. Silk they are harvesting from us, silk of name associations. Breath of Saturn on the windowpane. Paranoia as *parousia*.

Because these are the Elysian fields every travelogue
is a 'moonbeam of mahamudra'.

I had come over to watch the child while her parents were away. They brought me in to say hello to her. We had met a year before, in similar circumstances, but she was too young to remember that far back. She was diffident before me, an apparent stranger. So with looks and words and gestures I mimed for her the elaborate game we had played the last time I took care of her. Suddenly her eyes widened with delight: it's you! we're going to play that game again! —That is how it is for us each lifetime. Since we do not recognize him at first, he makes himself known to us by signs until we remember that we have dawdled with him before.

All true books say the same thing, but some go further. They give a method, a practice.

After midnight in a suburban bedroom I removed a drawer from a captain's bed and pulled out the metal box stashed beneath it. Then I reached back into the enclosure and felt around on the underside of a little ledge for the key that was taped there. In the box, wrapped in a *khatag*, was a spiral-bound notebook. I began to turn over its pages. On each recto was pasted an image; handwritten on the facing verso was a legend corresponding to it. The final image in the sequence was a photograph, cut out from a magazine, of a wall. It had been painted white, but other colors showed through in patches, as did the cement of which it was made. At its base a mantle of moss and dandelion lay across the reddish ground; here and there were rocks of various sizes, and, in a black plastic pot, a nettle was growing amid leaves of grass. I was in no doubt as to the subject of the photograph: it was that topos known to iconographers as 'a long time ago during a pause in a rain shower'. The man standing in front of the wall, who could be seen from the waist down, was wearing only flip-flops. When I looked over at the legend on the facing page, I saw that it seemed to have been left unfinished. 'The perfect dick', it read, 'doesn't exi'.

The enlightened master who is being summoned is not looking for imaginary support systems.

A Porphyrian tree can be retooled as a rhetorical device. Now you can use it to find topoi. 'Saints of our order' is a gloss of 'rosarium philosophorum'. 'Rosarium philosophorum' is for its part a gloss of 'Porphyrian tree'. A gloss is what is written 'for remembrance of the adventure'.

You are going to have to feel it all. But not all at once.

On a back road high above Death Valley we pulled over to stretch our legs. I scrambled up a ridge, the dog close behind me. At the top something came into view that hadn't been visible from the road. It looked like a temple naturally arisen from the side of the mountain, a rock grotto, a Marlinspike mandala. Like a portal to the Skellig Michael of the mind, to a shrine I'd heard a rumor of on the way to Ausangate, to the childhood home, in an unmade film of Pasolini's, of Paul of Tarsus. So I saw, looking across the slope at it. There was an outer and an inner gate, and in the center a kind of throne looking out over the valley. There I could fructify and volatilize the life essence. There I could attempt the interior adolescent ascent. There the 'boy reporter' and his foul-mouthed minotaur consort would sit in *yabyum*.

A memory palace is a place to wake up in, the 'si tacuisses' of consciousness. All memory palaces are built in the same space.

What *is* the 'Pleiadian agenda'?

A dance-craze conspiracy. Mass infection by eternal melody. World-music trance state.

The soundtrack for an imaginary *giallo*.

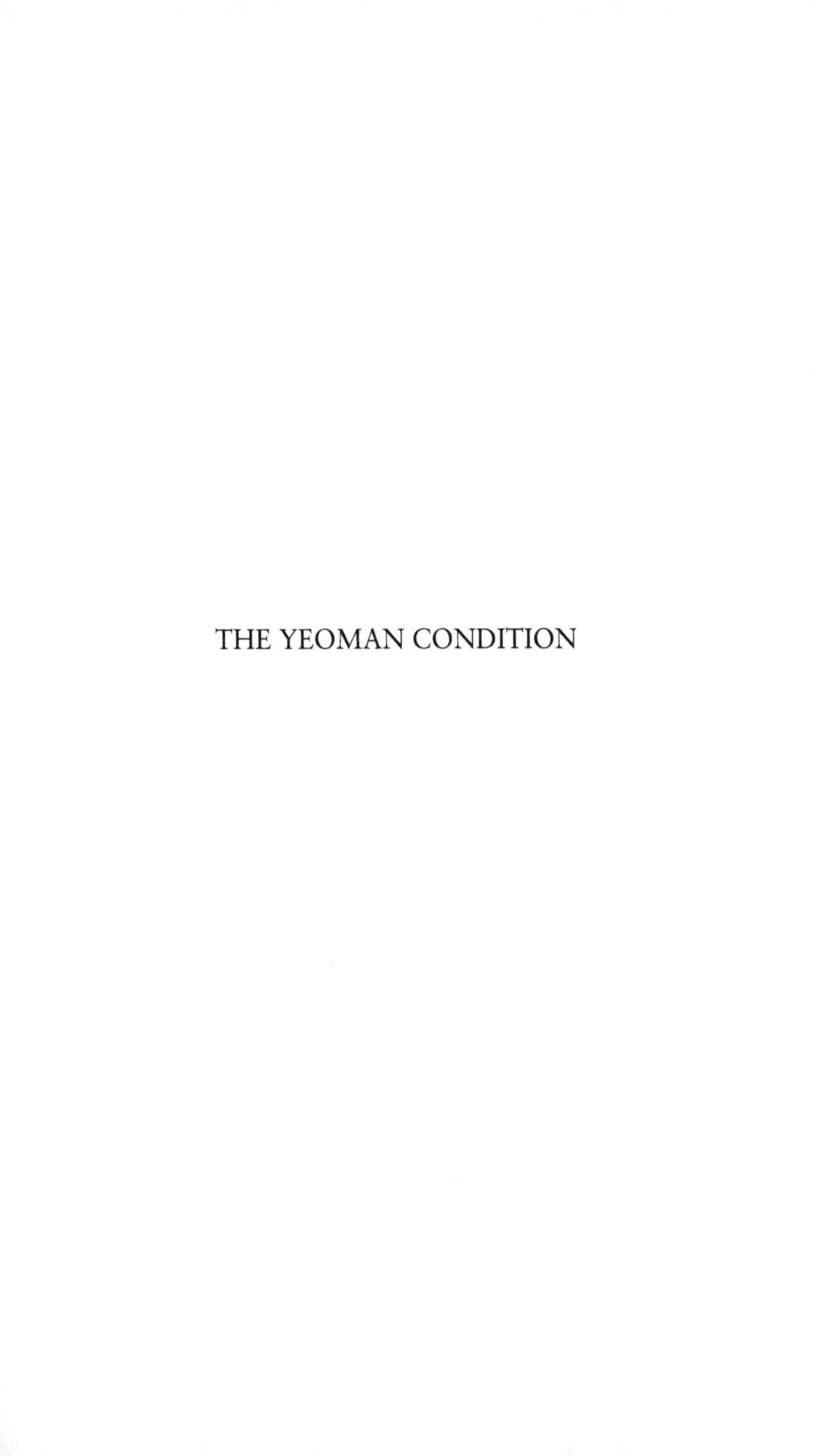

THE YEOMAN CONDITION

Books had been disappearing from the monastery library. There was never any sign that the lock on the door had been tampered with. I volunteered to spend a night in vigil there. Strange apparitions came, chimaeras. When I bared the symbol emblazoned on my breast they fled behind a shelf. I pulled out my dick and pissed all over them where they were hiding. Then I dragged the shelf away from the wall. In a crack between two bricks I found a book that had been missing for five hundred years.

Milk of the mirage. A rhino under a silk scarf. The task is to train yourself in what allows it to come through rather than to contrive a means of completing it.

When a book is read a certain way, it becomes liable to be read that way again. A chrestomathy of all its glosses. Which means that you can entrust things to it for safekeeping, sneak them in when no one's looking. My father told me a joke when I was eight or nine that I thought I would never recover from. It turned out to be true. 'Help, I'm trapped in a Chinese fortune-cookie factory.'

To give us a taste for the truth: the teacher's high calling. So we will remember that we are here to empty the hells and, eventually, the heavens. We sit at the feet of the *yogini* who addressed her questions to Origen of Alexandria in a letter. He answered: 'even the Devil is saved'. By her light we make out 'the string the pearls were strung on, the buried treasure, the figure in the carpet'. Our latter-day Origenism: we say that even the angels, even God himself is saved.

The Feuerbachian thesis is true, but only allegori-
cally.

An ark? A mirror for princes? A glass in which the sultan can examine his own backside? A booby trap, a cornerstone, a henge? A species that, ingested, allows for communication across *sambhogakaya* realms, *hurqalyas*? Just some unforgettable bit of buffoonery?

What I am looking for is a tombstone on which to garland my 'et in arcadia ego'.

A fairy tale whose 'hero' is the dew of sprightliness that condenses from the thin air of a particular imagination chamber. A thought-scene, with all its staffage, like 'the study' in a Jerome, 'the desert' in an Anthony, or 'the river' in a Christopher. The bare tree amid ruins to which they tied Sebastian when he underwent the sagittation.

From the other side of the curtain, the priestesses of our order cooed the mantra until I had it by heart. 'Chip chip de mantisque.' When I got back to my cell I transcribed it onto an index card, at the top of which I then wrote the number of the pigeonhole where I was accumulating material for a projected commentary on the odes to Nehumbraja, goatherd of Pitusirai.

Even when every copy has been destroyed, when everyone who has read or even just heard a rumor of it is buried in the ground, it will spontaneously regenerate itself, in one medium or another, on this planet or elsewhere, in every possible universe, until the end of time. That is why the would-be 'argonaut of awakening', setting out into the extinction event from wherever it is he finds himself, repurposes it (but this has always been its purpose) as a *vade mecum*, a little box in which to assemble a survival kit— a 'complete musical kit for all auspicious occasions'.

Spores, not seeds.

Pornographic illumination. A makeshift *sadhana*. 'Desire mind *is* nature mind.' A clerk in the court of love. To be reborn in Antinopolis!

Keeping a vow I'd made in the presence of a 'slutty Chenrezig' I went to recite the book on a mossy knoll above Deer Harbor. It was a *locus amoenus* I'd found decades before, with a hollow on top to sit in and on its flank a pile of rocks. One time I found some nudes from a magazine scattered amid the ferns there. This time I saw that someone had set up a branch like a bare flagpole in the pile of rocks.

The only instruction is to come to terms with the ob-
stacle.

My cell is a secret chamber in the glass castle projected holographically from the kernel of non-understanding that the book guards. I do my memory yoga there. It's just a matter of taking everything literally. Pulling out a card from the columbarium, admiring it, supplying it with the ever-present gloss.

'Sunyata' is an epithet of the spirit Mercurius.

A mantra is a *summula* of teachings in *dakini* language. You make it into a garland, as of severed heads. As of heads of garlic in a braid. Thus you preserve them for the season. Thus you adorn your mantle.

Leafing through the book, the *sadhaka* lays out a path of recollection. A path of recollection is an offering of a means of decreation to whoever might come across it, in order that mind might encounter mind, 'alone with the alone'. The legends are the remnants of an unbraiding of the image, a form of commentary in which the leavings of mind are followed back to mind itself. A path of crumbs is a kindness but primarily for the birds. A path of pebbles will be lost in underbrush or scattered before long. Blazes burn with the trees themselves. A labyrinth is guarded but some Theseus always comes. Which is why the *sadhaka* just loops a *khatag* through a nut, throws it, and goes where it lands.

'The gods must be crazy.' —But that's the quintessence of the ruse. For even in a god's dream mind is.

Late one night, age fifteen, a few friends and I were smoking cigarettes on a stoop. A man came down the sidewalk toward us muttering what sounded like obscenities. He was old, drunk, and filthy. He stopped directly in front of us and, without acknowledging the others, addressed himself to me. We knew where this was going; we knew his type. Then I met his eyes and—recognized him. There was no one there. Only patience, openness, and kindness beyond imagining. Nothing else mattered anymore, or had ever mattered. I looked further and further into his gaze. It never ended. My friends gaped at us, then tittered, then fell back embarrassed into silence. When we just kept looking they finally lost all interest and resumed a conversation from before.

I am not aware of having come into being.

A kind of lariat, a lasso. Just a bit of continuity looped over on itself. How does it not suffocate the one roped? What is the mechanism, and how do you learn the skill? —These are cattle-rustling questions. You know the name of the god of that trade.

In the gravesite I came across a cache of strange devices. I had no idea what they were for. I picked one up and turned it over in my hands in case the shape might tell me something. No such luck. I tried in vain to take as an instruction what had been written on the tombstone. So I wrapped it up and put it in my pack. Back in my cell I tried all my arts on it. I slept on it. I moped around. I wandered in search of old men and women who would know what it was for. I even found them. But finally I just had to fiddle with the thing until something happened.

THE LECTUARY OF SAN GAL DE NALGAS

Terrible falsity of every contrivance. Tell them what? That there is a book that fulfills all wishes? When it is much stranger than that.

The book is a map of topoi where it is possible to receive a transmission, 'ferne halwes'. —Fern hollows? —More or less. A vow can be taken to visit them. When this palace lies in ruins there will rise over the rubble a wormhole for the hollow body to return through.

I met a stranger on the road. Two emissaries, oblates in the same universal conventicle. We were 'on the qui vive'. Words passed between us. What we seemed to be talking about was not what we were talking about. But we weren't talking about anything else, either. Exchanging passwords, loafing in the shade of our perfect understanding, we whiled away the afternoon together.

A briar cage for the breath, a portable anchorhold. A song of realization. A canon I learned on my mother's lap. A melody for setting wisdom to.

A rainbow lightbody sitting cross-legged in interstellar space, sending out black searchlight beams from his eyes throughout the universe.

People don't necessarily want to hear about your
guru.

When I moved in I found an old trinket someone had left behind, intricately constructed and in exceedingly poor taste. I dusted it off and put it on the mantle. Every now and then I would pick it up and examine it. One time I must have been handling it less carefully than usual. Part of it cracked open and something fluttered to the floor. A slip of paper. When I picked it up I saw that there was writing on it, but I couldn't decipher it. It was just a bunch of disjointed words, only some of which I recognized. I glued the object back together and filed the slip of paper away. Then one day, in a flea market, I happened to see an identical trinket. I bought it at once, of course, took it home, and broke it in the same place I'd broken the other one. Something altogether different was written on the paper that I extracted, but it was equally uninterpretable. Time passed. One fine day I came across another one. Same story. How long was it before I figured out what would happen if I stacked the bits of paper on top of each other and held the little pile up to a source of light?

The labyrinth is made of our childhoods. The wedding is in Galilee. Everything remains in its place. The body is a memory palace, nothing more. A stained-glass window through which shines the lethal light: distraction. Divine distraction, full of love for its baby.

You don't sweep because there's dirt, you sweep because it's on your floor. —That's a meditation instruction.

Then in January I went treasure hiding on Toro Peak. The first day I followed an unmaintained road leading up toward the snowline. After several hours, having grown tired of walking, I pulled off my pack at a bend in the road and looked around for a flattish place to pitch my tent. I got up with the sun and, leaving everything there but a few necessary implements, bushwhacked around all day following birdcalls and deer trails and my sense of humor. When I came back to fix myself some dinner, I saw that, without meaning to, I'd set up camp the night before within a few dozen yards of an overgrown wishing ground, a little constellation of rocky outcrops. I made a spiral through its stations, picking out a processional route by which I hoped to unlock and activate it. At length I came to a formation that I can only call the cockpit. But hollowed out in that great rock was not just one seat, as I had grown accustomed to finding in such places, but six, and in their midst one more spot to stand in, as for a cluster of companions. A song was going through my head. One by one I assumed those seven posts, feeling around at each for its controls. The light grew purple. I looked out over the world. The next morning, before heading back down the mountain, I set up a cairn at the bend in the road.

I was alone in my cell. The window cast a square of light onto the wall. I lay on my bed with my hands folded behind my head. After a while I reached for the book. Onto an index card I transcribed the following lines: 'I have been alone here in your world. I have been without my brothers and sisters of the higher generation. At first I did not remember how to wake up into the dream we all inhabit on our other star. But I have cracked the case.' At the top of the card I wrote the number corresponding to the topos 'to know details only the [   ] would know'. The square of light moved up the wall.

A temple boy, a votary. 'The boy with the most beautiful asshole in the world.' People came from every land to gaze upon it, the 'very image of God'. It looked like a trema over the letter *c*.

A newspaper clipping: 'Says Scientist: We Ealreay Have the Antidote in Out Mist. It Floats in the Ether of the Almagest Pendragon Lambada.'

It appears that you don't have to be in a perpetually shitty mood.

You read the book so you can read the remnants of the book. You drink a cup of tea, and enjoy it, but what you read is the leaves that are left over. You do not read the tea. You do not drink the leaves. But first you have to let them settle.

'Mult asiïns, puns asiïns. / Puns asiïns, mult asiïns.'
—That's the recitation the *sadhaka* makes in closing,
to purify, seal, and dedicate the reading of the book.

Now to blazon all this, as for the engraver of a frontispiece. Behind a hinged bookshelf a little cell furnished with my implements, so many 'tools for finders'. On the desk a notebook is open to an image of a Porphyrian tree. Next to it a pen, a *mala*, and a pile of index cards. A little dog dreaming at my feet. There is an alembic, a cabinet gridded with pigeonholes, and a krater of green honey, overflowing. A postcard of the castle at Duino is taped to the wall above the mantle. Seven bees are flying in through the open window in a cluster; a mountain can be seen in the distance. My palms are cupped together, a leaf of grass taut between the thumbs.

The master of the oceanic thought appeared. He made a movement with his eyes. I looked in the direction he was indicating. And there it was. A wooden box in which an exoskeleton of light was folded up, like a praying mantis in a balsa coffin.

Zamboni wind.